What if we Run Out of Oil?

ck Hunter

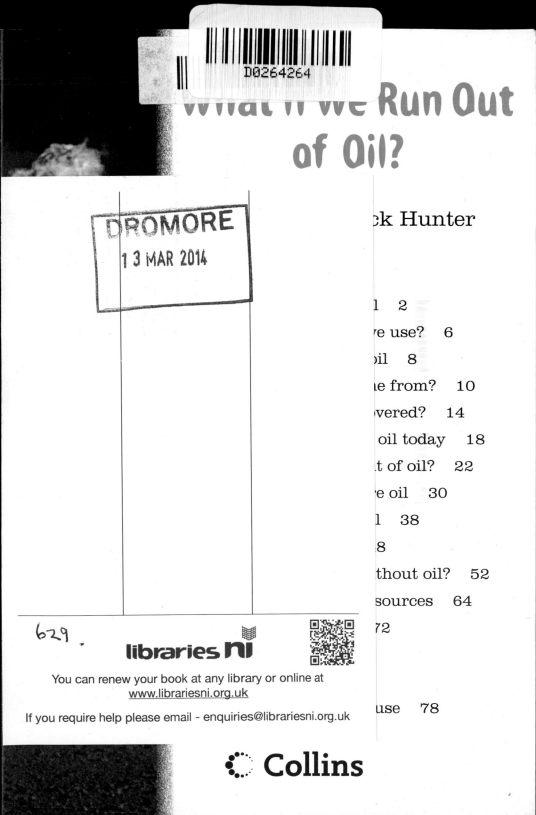

Collins

A world built on oil

How much oil have you used today? If you travelled to school by car or bus, the fuel that powered the vehicle was made from oil. If you cycled to school, your bike needs oil so that the wheels turn smoothly. You probably didn't get to school by plane, but if you did, planes need lots of fuel made from oil to keep them in the air.

Did you know?

Nine-tenths of the world's transport is powered by oil, from cars and motorcycles to massive container ships that carry goods around the world.

Even if you walked to school, you probably brought some oil with you. You may not be able to see the oil in your pens, your water bottle or your backpack, but these things all contain oil. Plastics and many other materials that we make come from oil.

Oil is everywhere around us. The fertilisers that help to grow our food are made out of oil. So are the chemicals used in cleaning products like washing-up liquid. The walls of our houses would have no paint on them without oil and all our clothes would have to be made from natural materials like wool and cotton instead of artificial materials that come from oil.

Living without oil

Try living for a day without using oil or products made from it. You'll have to think about lots of different areas of your life:

- You won't be able to wash your hair with shampoo in the morning – all the things we use to wash with are made using oil.

- If you need glasses you won't be able to wear them today. Plastic lenses and frames are made from oil.

- There are no cars today because you can't use petrol, so you'll have to walk to school.

- What about lunch? It may be impossible to find foods that didn't use oil to reach you. Food is carried to shops by ships, planes and trucks that all use oil.

- Playing football will be different too, with a heavy leather ball. You can't use a lighter plastic ball because it's made using oil.

- When you get home, there'll be no TV, video games or phones. They all include materials such as plastic, which come from oil.

Some things might be better in a world without oil. If we didn't have cars we would be fitter from walking everywhere. Life would certainly be very different.

How much oil do we use?

There are seven billion people in the world today and between us we use 30 billion **barrels** of oil each year. That's nearly five barrels of oil per year for every man, woman, and child on the planet.

That's an awful lot of oil, but the amount of oil we use is actually growing. This is partly because countries like China and India are becoming richer. As people get richer, they want to travel more and buy cars and many other things that use a lot of oil, such as televisions, computers, **disposable** goods and packaged food.

Not everyone uses a lot of oil. In **developing countries**, many people use wood as fuel for cooking, and travel on foot. They live without oil every day. They use more local, natural materials and grow their own food.

The biggest users of oil are still **developed countries** like the countries of western Europe, the USA and Australia.

Country	How much oil do they use in a year?
USA	25 barrels per person
Australia	17 barrels per person
UK	11 barrels per person
China	2 barrels per person
India	1 barrel per person
Bangladesh	1 barrel for every 5 people
Chad, Central Africa	1 barrel for every 20 people

Changing uses of oil

Changes on the road

As the number of cars in developed countries increased, people started to live further away from their work. They began to live in suburbs on the edge of cities that could only be reached by car. People started to shop at out-of-town shopping centres with a bigger choice of products and lots of parking rather than walk to local shops.

Changes in the air

Air travel uses a lot of oil. A Boeing 747 jumbo jet uses about 12 litres of fuel per kilometre. Air travel has grown in developed countries as flights have become more affordable for many people. Today billions of people travel by plane every year.

Changes in the way we use things

The petrochemical industry uses oil to create plastics and many other materials. Because plastics are so cheap, people in developed countries tend to throw things away rather than keeping and reusing them.

Some people can now work and study online from their own homes. This may mean that developed countries will use less oil for transport in future. But even if these countries are saving oil, other, less-developed countries will start to use more oil as their citizens get richer, travel more and buy more products.

Where does oil come from?

It's almost impossible for us to imagine a world without oil, but it's not so long since such a world existed. Oil has only become a vital part of our lives since the mid-1800s. However, the story of oil goes back a lot further than that.

Oil is made from the remains of tiny plants and animals. These living things died around 200 million years ago and their remains sank to the bottom of seas and lakes where they were covered with mud.

Over millions of years, new layers of rock crushed this layer of living or **organic matter**. It hardened into a layer of rock.

The crushed remains of prehistoric animals and plants are the ingredients needed to make oil. Then they have to be heated. Thousands of metres beneath Earth's crust, the rocks are hot enough to cook the organic matter. After a few million years of slow heating the plant and animal remains become liquid oil.

Oil only forms in sedimentary rock, which is made up of compressed layers of sand and other material. Once oil has formed, it will try to escape and rise through the rocks to the surface. Some rocks are permeable, meaning that oil and other liquids can pass through them. Others are impermeable – liquids can't pass through them. To be useful to us, oil has to be trapped underground by impermeable rock.

These sealed pockets in the rock are called oil traps. We can take the oil from the traps and use it.

How oil is formed

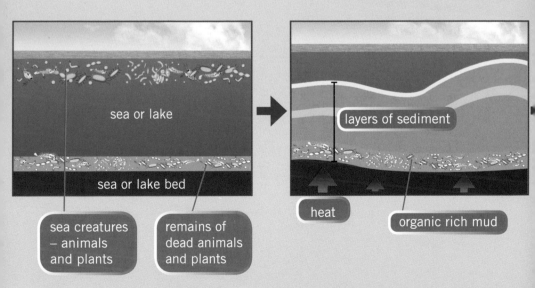

The conditions that are needed to create and trap oil only occur in some places. We know that much of the oil that has formed has seeped away to the Earth's surface or into the oceans. But we don't know exactly how much oil there is left under the ground or under the seabed, and until it's found and brought to the surface, we can only guess.

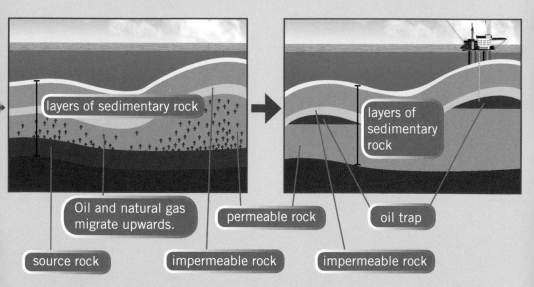

layers of sedimentary rock

layers of sedimentary rock

Oil and natural gas migrate upwards.

permeable rock

oil trap

source rock

impermeable rock

impermeable rock

When was oil discovered?

People have known about oil for thousands of years. Ancient people found lots of uses for oil that seeped from the ground. Oil was used in the surfaces of roads, as it still is today. In ancient Egypt and China, oil was used in medicine to cure burns and sores. In the mid-1800s, an American businessman called Patrick Keir sold "rock oil" that he claimed could cure everything from colds to blindness.

For thousands of years, people could only use the oil that seeped out of the ground. The ancient Chinese people developed early drills and pipes for getting more oil from under the ground, but these could not reach very far beneath the surface.

In 1846, the first **oil well** was drilled near Baku in Azerbaijan by mining engineer Fyodor Semyonov. In an oil well, a sharp drill attached to a pipe is used to tunnel into the rock to find oil. The first well struck oil 21 metres below the surface. Others followed, including the first oil well in North America in 1858.

An oil well

pipe

drill

oil

rock

the world's first oil wells in Baku, Azerbaijan

At the time of the first oil wells, oil was mainly used as fuel for oil lamps. As people started to use electric lights, there was less need for oil lamps. However, by then people had found a new use for oil: as fuel for the first cars, as well as ships and other engines. Oil had become a vital part of everyday life.

a filling station in Philadelphia, USA, in the early 20th century

Early oil **prospectors** thought that oil ran in underground rivers. As they found out more about how oil collected in traps, oil was found in more places. Technology also made it possible to explore new places, and scientists found new ways to pinpoint exactly where to drill for oil.

Did you know?

Before the first oil wells were drilled, fuel for oil lamps came from sperm whales, which have a thick layer of oily blubber. Demand for their oil was so high that the number of sperm whales fell sharply in the 1800s.

Finding and using oil today

Oil is found in areas called oilfields. In these areas, the types and formations of rock are exactly right to store large amounts of oil. Areas of rock containing oil are called "oil reservoirs". The rock is porous, meaning it has tiny holes in it that liquid oil collects in, a bit like a sponge filled with water. When an oil well drills into this spongy rock, the thick, black oil naturally rises to the top of the well. Many oil reservoirs are several kilometres underground.

2 Canada

7 Venezuela

Oil is not spread evenly around the world. Some countries have lots of oil beneath their land or beneath the seabed close to their coasts; others have little or no oil. Countries with the largest amounts, or reserves, of oil include Saudi Arabia, Iran, Iraq and the United Arab Emirates around the Arabian Gulf. Canada, Venezuela, Nigeria and Russia also have large oil reserves.

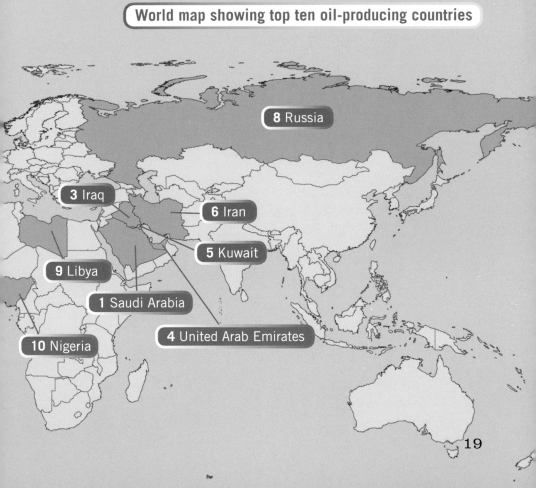

World map showing top ten oil-producing countries

8 Russia

3 Iraq

6 Iran

5 Kuwait

9 Libya

1 Saudi Arabia

10 Nigeria

4 United Arab Emirates

Making oil useful

Oil is not ready to use as soon as it comes out of the ground. The black liquid that is pumped to the surface is called **crude oil**. It contains many different substances, each of which has a different use.

Oil also needs to be moved to where it will be used. Oil from the Arabian Gulf may be moved to Europe, North America or China. The oil is transported by ships called oil tankers or by **pipelines** to a **refinery** closer to where it will be used.

At the oil refinery, chemical processes separate the crude oil into different substances, which we use for different things. Most of a barrel of crude oil is used to make fuel for cars, planes and ships. Only a small part is used to create plastics and all the other things we make from oil.

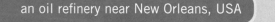

an oil refinery near New Orleans, USA

Where does a barrel of crude oil go?

- petrol
- diesel
- aircraft fuel
- gas
- solid fuel
- fuel oil
- gas that turns to liquid
- asphalt, a sticky material used in roadbuilding
- other products including plastics
- lubricants which can be used in engine oil

Are we running out of oil?

Renewable materials are materials that can easily
be replaced. Plants that we use for food are one example:
if we eat them we can always grow some more.
There are also renewable sources of energy that we
can use without worrying that they will run out one
day such as energy from the Sun, which is captured by
solar panels.

Oil is a **non-renewable** material. The natural process of making oil takes millions of years and there is a limited supply. Many scientists are concerned that we rely too much on oil for our energy needs.

Up until now, oil has been plentiful and new oil has been discovered regularly. But however much oil we discover, we know that once it is used we cannot replace it. What we don't know is when we will have used it all.

How long will it last?

There are different views about how much oil we have left. Oil is not likely to run out next week. If we keep using the same amount of oil as we use now, there is enough oil already discovered to last for 50 years. If we continue to use more oil every year, it won't last as long.

Did you know?

Use of oil in developing countries is likely to increase 2.5 times by 2020. Worldwide demand for electricity to power things such as televisions and computers will increase by 70% over the same period. Many countries produce the electricity they need using power stations that burn oil.

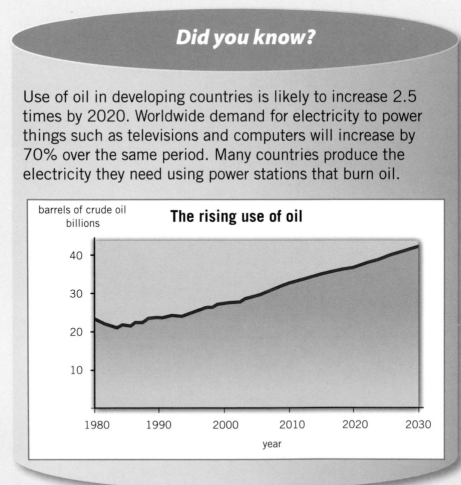

barrels of crude oil
billions

The rising use of oil

year

Oil for the future

We are finding new sources of oil all the time.
The problem with these new sources of oil is that no one
knows how much more there is to find.

drilling for oil on an oil rig in Alberta, Canada

What if we keep using the same amount of oil?

We may not be about to run out of oil but most experts agree that several things will happen if we continue to use oil at the same rate as we do now.

Many scientists believe that at some point oil production will start to decline.
There will be fewer new discoveries.
It will become more difficult to get oil from older oilfields. A bit like when you wring out a wet cloth, at first it is very easy to get oil from an oilfield, but it gets more difficult to squeeze out the last few drops. What experts can't agree on is whether this peak has already been reached.

If oilfields produce less oil, or it gets more expensive to take oil out of the ground, this will affect the price of oil. If people are still using the same amount of oil, there will be more people trying to buy each barrel of oil. The price will rise. This is called the law of supply and demand.

former oil fields being used for a school in Baku, Azerbaijan

27

Rising prices

If oil prices rise around the world, it won't just affect car drivers or air travellers. The price of oil affects how much we pay for almost everything.

- A wide range of items – from cleaning products to toys – are made from oil.

- Other things are sold to you in plastic packaging that is made from oil. Many foods are packaged in plastic to protect them and the cost of the packaging is included in the price you pay.

- All products have to be delivered to the shop by lorry and they may have come by plane or ship from another continent. All of this transport uses oil.

When oil prices rise, the price of food in markets around the world goes up.

If the oil price rises, the cost of all things made from and transported by oil will also go up

Oil companies and countries that produce oil are happy because they make more money if prices rise. But they can have problems if the price gets too high – people may use less oil, for example by switching to smaller cars.

Did you know?

The price of oil affects food prices around the world as the costs of fertilisers and transport rise. This has a big impact in developing countries where people have less money for food.

The search for more oil

The oil companies and governments that keep the world supplied with oil know that they need to keep finding new sources of oil as old ones are used up. Technology is becoming more and more important in this search.

Underground mapping

Geologists search for rocks that contain oil. In seismic surveys, pulses of sound are transmitted into the ground. Using the echoes that come back from different layers of rock, geologists can build a computer model of the rocks deep underground. They look for rock formations where oil could be trapped.

Although geologists can find possible oilfields, the only way to be sure there's oil is to drill a well. This well could be several kilometres deep and take months to drill. The costs of drilling are huge.

The people hunting for oil know that many of the biggest and most accessible oilfields in the world, like the ones in Saudi Arabia, have already been discovered. New technology means they can now look for oil in places that were too remote or dangerous a few years ago.

This computer model from a seismic survey uses different colours to show various types of rock. Geologists know that some rock formations are more likely to contain oil.

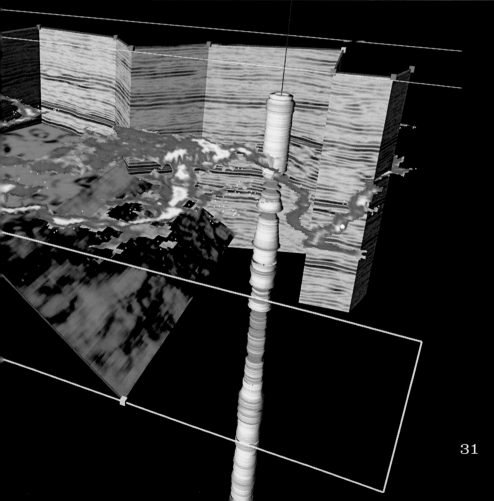

Deep-sea oil drilling

Drilling for oil beneath the seabed is nothing new. For many years, oil workers have worked on offshore oil platforms.

However, until the 1990s, most experts thought that it was impossible to drill for oil in waters deeper than 450 metres. Ocean currents, **water pressure** and extreme cold on the seabed would make deep drilling very difficult. Satellite-controlled engines now keep oil rigs in position while robot submarines maintain equipment in the deep ocean.

an oil rig in the North Sea, off the coast of the UK

New technologies like this have now made it possible to drill in water more than 3,000 metres deep.

Deep-water drilling has uncovered new oilfields in areas like the Gulf of Mexico, off the coast of Brazil, and in the deep waters west of the UK's Shetland Islands. However, these new deep-water oilfields still make up only a fraction of the world's oil reserves. This oil costs much more to extract than oil on land or in shallow water because the technology is more complicated and insurance costs are higher.

Did you know?

Many of the countries that use the most oil, such as the USA, the European Union and China have to buy it from other countries. These countries are keen to find more oil of their own, even if getting oil from these sources is difficult or dangerous.

Oil sands

Oil companies are not just looking for oil beneath the sea. There are other opportunities that might help to meet the world's need for oil.

Canada has nearly as much oil as Saudi Arabia, but it is much more difficult to get at. This oil is found in areas called oil sands. This form of oil is not liquid but almost solid and it is mixed with sand. Oil sands are not deep underground but often close to the surface. They are mined in huge open pits.

This huge facility, in Alberta, Canada, extracts oil from oil sands.

Oil sands are an expensive source of oil. A lot of energy and water is needed to turn oil sands into liquid oil that can be refined. Around two tonnes of oil sand is needed to make just one barrel of oil, which means that creating billions of barrels of oil from this source will destroy huge areas of land.

If we can overcome these problems, getting oil from oil sands could provide us with enough oil to meet our needs for many years to come. Extracting this oil is expensive now, but the costs are likely to come down as oil companies learn the best ways to process this kind of oil.

Oil in the Arctic

There are few places left on Earth where people have not yet looked for oil. In their quest to find more oil, explorers are now looking in places that are almost untouched by humans. Oil has been found in Alaska in the far north of North America and there is now a race to find oil in the Arctic.

One of the biggest problems in the Arctic is the extreme cold. For much of the year, the ocean is covered with thick ice and drilling for oil is impossible. Even in the warmer months, drifting icebergs have to be towed away by ships so they don't damage oil rigs.

The Arctic is also home to many species of wildlife not found anywhere else and there are worries that oil exploration would affect them.

However, many governments and oil companies believe that drilling for oil in such an extreme environment is the best way to find more oil. Many people who live in the region, for example in Greenland, would welcome the oil industry and the jobs and money it brings.

Did you know?

There's one continent where there is no oil exploration. Antarctica is covered by a sheet of ice more than two kilometres thick. Although many believe that large oil reserves lie beneath the Antarctic ice, an international agreement prevents drilling for oil in this fragile wilderness to protect it.

The trouble with oil

Damaging animals and plants

The Arctic is not the only place where oil causes problems for plants, animals and people. Oil spills do great damage to the natural world.

When oil is spilt on water, it rises to the surface and forms a sticky film on the sea. Sea creatures and birds that come into contact with this oily sludge will be covered in oil. Oil prevents birds from flying. When they try to clean themselves, they will swallow poisonous oil. The lucky ones will be rescued and cleaned up by relief workers, but many will never recover.

Oil can damage plants and animals in delicate habitats like rivers and coastal areas for many years. In 1989, the *Exxon Valdez* tanker ran aground in Alaska. This had a huge impact on seabirds and other wildlife. If one species of plant or animal dies, that can change the balance of the entire habitat – a source of food for another species may have disappeared. Oil is broken up by bacteria over time but this takes much longer in cold **climates** like Alaska.

Did you know?

Scientists believe that the chemicals used to clean up oil spills are almost as damaging as the oil itself. Oil stays on the surface, so does less damage to underwater life, but chemical **dispersants** can harm underwater coral.

This otter survived the *Exxon Valdez* oil spill in Alaska, but other marine wildlife was badly affected.

Oil spills

Many of the worst oil-spill disasters have happened when oil is being transported to where it will be refined or used.

Oil tankers carry large quantities of oil across the world's oceans. They are huge ships and, if they run aground in bad weather, oil spills into the sea or directly on to the coast. Oil can also leak from pipelines on land.

clean-up operations after the *Exxon Valdez* disaster in Alaska, in 1989

The World's Biggest Oil Spills

1967   *Torrey Canyon* tanker spill. The UK's biggest oil disaster –
        117,000 tonnes of oil spilled, 15,000 sea birds killed.

1979   Oil-well explosion, Mexico. The biggest accidental
        oil disaster until 2010 – 475,000 tonnes of oil spilled.

oil burning in the aftermath of
the Mexican oil-well explosion

1979   *Atlantic Empress* tanker collides with another ship in
        the Caribbean. The world's biggest tanker disaster –
        287,000 tonnes of oil spilled.

1989   *Exxon Valdez* tanker disaster, Alaska – 43,000 tonnes of
        oil spilled.

1991   Arabian Gulf oil spill – the world's worst oil disaster.
        Iraqi troops deliberately released 1.5 million tonnes
        of oil into the sea during the Gulf War to block the waters
        to enemy ships.

2010   *Deepwater Horizon* disaster. The world's biggest accidental
        spill – up to 670,000 tonnes of oil spilled.

Disaster in the Gulf of Mexico

The *Deepwater Horizon* oil spill was the world's biggest ever accidental spill. It began when there was an explosion on the *Deepwater Horizon* oil rig on 20 April 2010, starting a fire that burnt out of control for 36 hours. Finally the rig turned over and sank to the bottom of the Gulf of Mexico. The rig had been drilling a new oil well in 1,500 metres of water when the explosion happened.

The blast killed 11 people, and many more had to be rescued from the rig by helicopter. This was only the beginning of the *Deepwater Horizon* disaster that would become the world's worst accidental oil spill.

fire boats tackling the flames on the *Deepwater Horizon* rig

skimming boats collecting surface oil from the *Deepwater Horizon* oil spill

Between April and July 2010, around 670,000 tonnes of oil gushed from the ruptured well on the ocean floor, forming a massive oil slick on the surface.

A fleet of ships worked to clean up the oil and prevent it reaching the wetland habitats of the Gulf coast.

Engineers on drilling ships and robot submarines beneath the waves tried to plug the leak more than a kilometre below them.

When the flow of oil was stopped almost three months after the disaster, local people and wildlife were left to count the cost. The long-term effects may not be known for many years but we can get a good idea from the impact of previous oil disasters.

43

Caught up in the oil business

Oil can also do a lot of good. Countries that make money from oil often use this money for projects that benefit a lot of people, like building roads and hospitals and providing water supplies.

However, in some countries the land and the people who live there are affected in less positive ways by the search for oil. While some benefit from the jobs and wealth associated with oil, others are affected by pollution and the change in land use.

The Niger Delta in Nigeria is a rich source of oil. Major oil companies drill in this region and Nigeria's government has benefited from this natural resource for over 100 years.

The Ogoni people who live in the Delta have not been happy about the search for oil there. They argue that pollution from oil has damaged the environment of the region and made their farmland unusable. While the discovery of oil in Nigeria has helped some, it has not been so beneficial for others.

Oil pollution

Oil spills make headlines but they make up only a small part of the oil that gets into rivers and other habitats. The oil that leaks from vehicles on to the roads of a large city every year could be as much as an oil spill from a tanker.

Many plastic products made from oil cannot be broken down in nature in the same way as natural materials such as wood. We throw away plastic drink bottles and food containers but they do not decay. People are now having to think of new ways to deal with this rubbish, such as recycling – but not all plastic is easy to recycle.

When oil is burnt, it releases fumes into the **atmosphere**.
These fumes are made of particles of oil that has not fully
burnt and gases that come from the burnt oil. The fumes
combine with water in the air to create acid rain that
damages buildings and kills trees.

Even more worrying is the effect that fumes from
burning fossil fuels are having on Earth's climate.

Climate change

The Earth's temperature is rising. This is causing
extreme weather events, such as floods and droughts.
Most scientists believe that our appetite for burning
fossil fuels including coal, oil and gas is actually
changing Earth's climate. This is because burning fossil
fuels produces a gas called **carbon dioxide**.
The amount of this gas in Earth's atmosphere has
increased by about one third in the last 250 years.

Carbon dioxide is known as a **"greenhouse gas"**. Greenhouse gases in Earth's atmosphere allow light and heat from the Sun to reach Earth. They also stop much of this heat from escaping, making the planet warm enough for plants and animals, including humans. If there are too many greenhouse gases, too much heat from the Sun is trapped, in what is called a "greenhouse effect". This causes Earth's climate to get warmer.

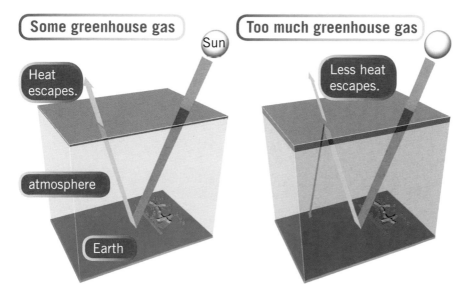

An international report on climate change has predicted that temperatures around the world could rise by up to four degrees Centigrade over the next century if we continue to burn fossil fuels at the same rate as we do now.

What will climate change mean?

You might think it wouldn't be a bad thing to have warmer weather. However, warmer weather around the world will make life much more difficult for all of us.

Rising sea levels

The land and sea in the regions close to the North and South Poles are covered in thick sheets of ice that are several kilometres thick in places. If the climate continues to warm up, this ice would melt. If ice that is currently on land melts into the sea, this would cause the levels of seas around the world to rise. Low-lying areas including many coastal cities would be flooded.

Deserts and droughts

As the climate gets warmer, many areas with hot climates will become so hot that no plants will grow and more areas will become desert. Crop failures and droughts will take away the only source of food and water for some of the world's poorest people.

Did you know?

Millions of people live on the edges of deserts or on fertile ground around the world's great rivers. Rising sea levels and droughts will affect these people the most, although many of them hardly use oil or other fossil fuels.

How can we live without oil?

There are two main ways we can reduce our reliance on oil. The first is to do fewer of the things that use oil. The second is to find alternative fuels that do the same job as oil but don't cause the same problems.

Travel

Most oil is used for transport. One way to reduce our use of oil would be to cut the number of cars on the road and the amount we use them.

Governments use different methods to persuade people to use their cars less:

● Improve public transport: if we can get to work or school more quickly and cheaply we may leave the car at home.

- Make cycling and walking easier: exercise is good for our health, and more cycle paths will encourage people to use bikes.

- Make driving more expensive: putting extra **taxes** on fuel encourages people to drive less.

- Give people reasons to share their cars: special lanes on roads can be set aside for car sharers so they will get to work more quickly.

Of course, cars are not the only form of transport that uses oil. Cheap air travel has meant more carbon dioxide **emissions** from aircraft. High-speed trains can replace aircraft over shorter distances, use less fuel and release less carbon dioxide. In China, the world's fastest train travels between Beijing and Shanghai at over 480 kilometres per hour.

Clean cars

Technology can also help us to use less oil. If we can develop cars that don't use oil, that would be a big step in ending our reliance on oil.

Hybrid cars are a move in the right direction. They run on an electric motor alongside a petrol engine to reduce the amount of fuel they use. When driving on a flat road at a constant speed, the petrol engine works on its own and charges the electric motor. When the car needs extra power, such as when going uphill or in a city where the car keeps stopping and starting, the electric motor helps out.

Hybrid cars have electric engines, but they still need petrol in order to run.

Other ways to run cars

Biofuels are also starting to be used to power cars. These fuels are made from plants and can be mixed with petrol and diesel for use in vehicles.

If we use more biofuels and hybrid cars this will help to reduce the amount of oil we use. They're not the perfect solution to climate change as they still release some carbon dioxide and use some oil. Scientists and companies are also looking at other options for cleaner cars, including electric cars running on batteries and cars powered by **hydrogen**. Hydrogen cars produce energy from a reaction between hydrogen and oxygen. The main waste product from this is water.

Major car companies are developing cleaner cars but most cars sold are still powered by petrol and diesel. Why are cleaner cars not more popular?

- Cost: cleaner cars cost more to buy than conventional cars, although by using less oil, they should save money over time.

- Performance: electric and hydrogen cars can't travel as far or as fast as petrol cars yet.

- Refuelling: cars that run on electricity or hydrogen need regular recharging or refuelling. The problem is that there are very few places to do this at present.

This electric car, built in 2008, can travel up to 180 kilometres before it has to recharge its batteries.

Biofuels also have problems, for example they need lots of space to grow. If more land is used to grow plants for biofuels, there will be less land to grow food for people. When they are burnt, biofuels also release greenhouse gases, just like oil. But on the other hand, while these plants are growing they absorb carbon dioxide from the atmosphere. This means they help to reduce the amount of greenhouse gases, too.

The drawbacks mean that it will be a while before clean cars take over from petrol- and diesel-fuelled cars and become a common sight on our roads.

Did you know?

There are expected to be 2.9 billion vehicles on the world's roads by 2050 – nearly three times as many as there are now. By that time, there will probably be much less oil available for fuel.

Food and clothing miles

Another way to reduce how much oil we use is to think about the things we buy. We can check where they came from and think about how much oil was used to get them to our local supermarket.

Many fruits and vegetables travel by air to keep them fresh. People are used to having their favourite foods available all the year round, even if they are usually only available in one season in their own country. But it takes a lot of oil to transport this food. Eating locally produced food means less oil will be used. Certain produce may not be available all year round but eating different foods in each season adds lots of variety to meals.

SARAH GREEN'S OR

SOIL ASSOCIATION · ORGANIC STANDARD

TILLINGHAM GROWN SEASONAL OR

Beans on sale in supermarkets may
have come all the way from Kenya.

Some environmental campaigners say that worrying
about how far your food has travelled is not
the whole story. In developed countries farmers often
use fertilisers that are produced using oil and their
produce is usually sold in plastic packaging.

Fossil fuel alternatives

For many years, natural gas was seen as an almost worthless product that had to be dealt with when drilling for oil. Gas is made in the same way as oil and is often found in the same places. It is gas rather than liquid because it is older and has been cooked underground for longer.

In recent years, gas has become more important as an alternative to oil. It is used more than oil for generating power and is used as fuel in a wide range of vehicles from buses to cars.

This ship carries liquid natural gas. It can only unload at ports fitted with ultra-cold storage tanks, to keep the gas in its liquid form.

Gas has some advantages over oil:

- When gas is burnt it produces more energy than oil. It also produces fewer greenhouse gases.

- Gas does not cause as much pollution and damage to plants and animals if it is spilt.

- Gas is more plentiful than oil, although it is also a non-renewable fossil fuel.

- Compressed natural gas in a cylinder can be used to power vehicles.

The main drawbacks with gas are that it can explode, and it is more difficult to transport. Gas can be transported in liquid form but has to be kept at a very low temperature and carried in special ships.

The nuclear option

Nuclear energy is produced when the core of an atom is broken apart. Atoms are tiny particles from which everything in the Universe is made. Splitting up complex atoms releases huge amounts of energy.

Many people see nuclear energy as the best way to make electricity without using fossil fuels. Nuclear energy relies on **radioactive** materials, like the metal uranium. Although these radioactive materials are non-renewable, they are used in quite small quantities compared with fossil fuels.

Most nuclear energy is used in power stations, although submarines and naval ships have been powered by nuclear reactors, meaning that they can remain at sea for long periods without needing to be refuelled in port.

a nuclear power station

Accidents at nuclear power stations can have dangerous consequences, releasing radioactive steam into the air.

The big problem with nuclear power is that radioactive materials can be very dangerous if they are released into the environment. Invisible radiation from this fuel can poison land and water for hundreds of years. This makes disposal of it difficult and plans include storing the waste deep underground for 1,000 years.

The ultimate solution to our energy needs could be nuclear fusion. This is how the Sun generates energy by fusing simple atoms. Nuclear fusion creates huge amounts of energy but without creating radioactive waste. It will be many years before scientists can create a working fusion reactor.

Renewable energy sources

Energy from the Sun

All energy on Earth originally comes from the Sun. Solar energy is energy that comes directly from the Sun's rays. It can be captured using solar panels.

The Sun's energy also drives the world's weather systems. These weather systems generate huge amounts of energy, for example in the wind that drives a sailing boat or waves that crash against the coast. Wind and wave energy can be used to make electricity.

The Sun's heat also makes water evaporate from oceans and fall as rain on higher ground. Water then moves downhill in streams and rivers. Engineers create **hydroelectric** power when they build dams and capture the energy of this water flowing downhill.

Unlike oil, all of these energy sources are renewable and will never run out. The difficult thing is capturing the energy from them.

Did you know?

In 2010, an experimental plane powered by the Sun's rays through the solar panels on its 61-metre wingspan landed safely after 26 hours in the air. Some of the solar energy was stored in batteries so the plane could keep flying during the night. The plane has wings the size of a large passenger aircraft but can only carry the pilot. Passenger flights using solar power are still a long way off.

a hydroelectric dam in Oregon, USA

All forms of renewable energy have positive and negative aspects to them. The big benefit of renewable energies generated from the Sun's heat and weather systems is that these energies do not produce any greenhouse gases.

There is enough energy from the Sun to supply all our energy needs. However, this energy is spread out across the surface of the Earth. Even in the sunniest parts of the world, huge areas covered by solar panels that convert sunshine to electricity are needed to provide the same energy we get from fossil fuels.

Energy from the wind

Wind energy is cheap and plentiful but we can
only harness a tiny amount of the total available.
Huge numbers of wind turbines are needed to generate
large amounts of energy, and they only work in places
where winds are strong and constant, such as coastal
areas or offshore. Wind turbines are also noisy and can
harm birds.

Water power

Water or hydroelectric power is the most widely used renewable energy for generating electricity. Water flowing towards the sea in rivers can generate large amounts of energy, but building dams to harness this energy is expensive and involves flooding large areas of land. The energy in waves and tides can also be captured, although this is much more difficult.

Geothermal energy

When a volcano erupts we can see the heat that is under the Earth's surface. This heat beneath Earth's crust can be used to heat water and produce steam to drive turbines. In some places, super-heated water is naturally present underground. **Geothermal** energy is already used in volcanic areas such as Iceland.

This power station near Reykjavik harnesses Iceland's geothermal energy reserves to produce electricity.

Geothermal power stations are costly to build and this power is easier to use in volcanic areas, so it's not a very global energy source. Scientists are also unsure about the long-term impact of using this type of energy. Taking too much heat energy from some areas could make it less effective over time.

Sun, wind, water and geothermal energy can generate electricity, which can be used to charge batteries for electric vehicles. But these forms of energy can't be used directly as a fuel for vehicles.

Can renewable energy replace oil?

It will be some time before these renewable energies are able to replace the power that we currently get from fossil fuels. Scientists need to keep looking for new sources of renewable energy as demand grows and oil supplies decline. Even big oil companies have **invested** in alternative energy sources, although the money involved is much less than they spend looking for new sources of oil.

Energy conservation

Finding ways to use less energy is just as important as finding new sources of energy. Much of the energy we use is wasted. For example, many of our homes do not have enough insulation to keep heat inside them. We use electricity when we leave televisions, computers and other appliances on standby rather than turning them off. If we can use less energy overall, it will help to reduce our reliance on oil and other fossil fuels.

an energy-saving light bulb

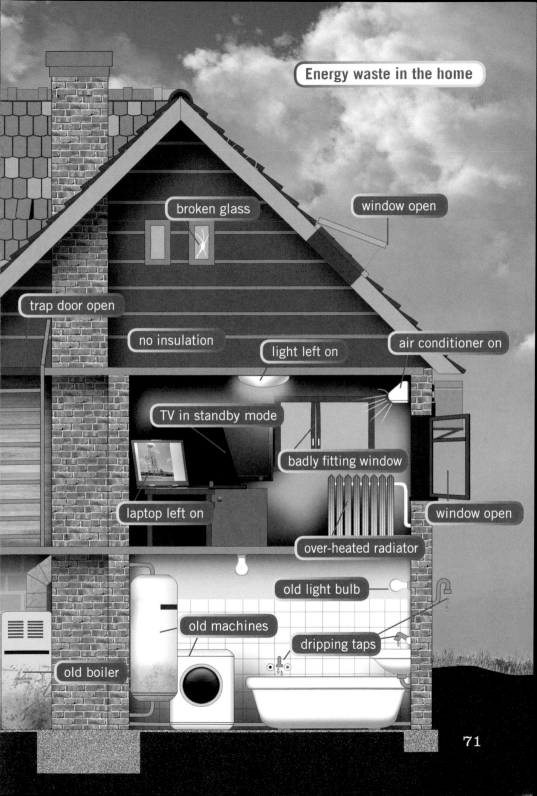

Can we change?

We need to change the way we live in many ways if we are going to use less oil and slow the pace of climate change. The question is, can we change in time?

There are already many examples of people and governments developing plans to use less oil. Cities around the world have started to introduce buses powered by natural gas and biodiesel and many countries have invested in green technologies. Here are a few examples:

- Formula 1 cars use a lot of fuel, travelling less than a mile for every litre of fuel used. The sport has announced plans to reduce engine emissions by half, without affecting the performance of the cars. Maybe this will convince people that a cleaner car is not necessarily a slower car.

solar panels in Liwa desert, Abu Dhabi

- Abu Dhabi has been called the richest city in
  the world. It has become rich because of the huge
  oil reserves found beneath its desert sands.
  In 2010, Abu Dhabi announced plans to build
  the world's largest solar energy plant. The cloudless
  skies are ideal for capturing solar energy and
  Abu Dhabi hopes to become less dependent on oil
  in future.

- Wind turbines are a common sight in many
  countries. Denmark produces about one-fifth of its
  electricity from wind power.

If scientists are right about climate change, and if oil gradually becomes less plentiful and more expensive, we will all have to change how we use oil. We also need to be aware that the problems we face are global. Climate change will not stop if you, or even everyone in your city or country, stops using fossil fuels. Everyone around the world needs to do the same.

Oil has helped to create the modern world, but its use has also led to pollution of many of the planet's wild places. Most seriously, it has contributed to a change in climate that could affect life on Earth as we know it.

Some people still believe that our use of fossil fuels is not causing climate change. Most scientists disagree with them. However, no one can deny that oil is a non-renewable source of energy. One day we will have to live without it. We don't know when this will be but we need to start planning for a life without oil.

These eco-friendly houses use 81% less energy for heating than ordinary homes nearby.

Glossary

atmosphere	the layer of gases surrounding a planet
barrels	units of measurement for oil. One barrel equals just under 160 litres.
carbon dioxide (CO_2)	a gas released when products containing carbon, including oil, are burnt in air. Carbon dioxide is also released when animals and plants breathe.
climates	the usual weather found in particular places
crude oil	the substance that is taken out of the ground in oil exploration. Crude oil is refined to make many different oil-based products.
developed countries	countries like the USA and Japan, where people are comparatively wealthy and buy a lot of products
developing countries	countries where people are less wealthy, and don't buy many products, or are just starting to buy more products
dispersants	chemicals applied to oil to break it up into drops
disposable	usually thrown away after one or two uses
emissions	things that are released, e.g. emissions of carbon dioxide into the atmosphere
geologists	people who study rocks and the Earth's surface
geothermal	coming from heat generated under the ground
greenhouse gas	any of the gases that contribute to the greenhouse effect and climate change. Carbon dioxide is a greenhouse gas.

hydroelectric	to do with electricity generated by the energy of water flowing downstream
hydrogen	the most common element in the galaxy. It usually appears as a colourless, odourless gas.
invested	put money into something, such as a business, with the hope of making more money
non-renewable	unable to be replaced once it has been used
oil well	a hole drilled in the ground or seabed to access oil
organic matter	matter that was once a living thing and that breaks down as it decays
pipelines	series of pipes that can be used to transport oil and other liquids and gases across land and under the sea
prospectors	people who search for new sources of oil
radioactive	emitting tiny particles called radiation, which can damage human and animal health
refinery	an industrial plant where crude oil is separated into different materials
renewable	able to be replaced. Plants are renewable, as is the energy that comes from the Sun.
solar	from or to do with the Sun
taxes	money that people pay to the government, which the government uses to provide services like schools and hospitals
water pressure	pressure applied by water. Pressure is higher at greater depths.

Index

solar panels for heating

growing your own fruit

working from home

double-glazed windows

TV turned off

growing your own vegetables

:paw: Ideas for reading :paw:

Written by Clare Dowdall BA(Ed), MA(Ed)
Lecturer and Primary Literacy Consultant

Learning objectives: understand underlying themes, causes and points of view; sustain engagement with longer texts using different techniques to make the text come alive; use the techniques of dialogic talk to explore ideas, topics or issues; select words and language drawing on their knowledge of literary features and formal and informal writing; integrate words, images and sounds imaginatively for different purposes

Curriculum links: Science: Enquiry in environmental and technological contexts; Geography: What's in the news?

Interest words: fertilizers, chemicals, prospectors, reservoirs, crude oil, pipelines, refinery, renewable, geologists, seismic surveys, frontiers, hydrogen, nuclear energy, radioactive, uranium, hydroelectric power, geothermal energy

Resources: ICT, whiteboard

Getting started

This book can be read over two or more reading sessions.

- Ask children to discuss what they already know about oil, suggesting what oil is used for and where they think it comes from.

- Look at the front cover and read the blurb together. Ask children to explore their ideas about what will happen if we run out of oil. Encourage them to listen to and question each other, writing a list on the whiteboard of information they would like to know about oil.

Reading and responding

- Ask children to read to p5. Explore their reactions to the notion of living a day without oil, and how they would cope.

- Focus on the chart on p7 and ask children to speculate why oil use is heavier in Australia and the USA, than the UK, e.g. due to the size of the country.

- Ask children to read to the end of the book, looking for and making notes on the problems associated with oil as an energy source, e.g. prices may rise and it might run out.